WIMBLEDON
FACTS, FIGURES
& FUN

CAMERON BROWN

*"Any book without a mistake in it has had
too much money spent on it"*
Sir William Collins, publisher

WIMBLEDON
FACTS, FIGURES
& FUN

CAMERON BROWN

ff&f

Wimbledon
Facts, Figures & Fun

Published in Great Britain and USA by
Facts, Figures & Fun, an imprint of
AAPPL Artists' and Photographers' Press Ltd.
10 Hillside, London SW19 4NH, UK
info@ffnf.co.uk; www.ffnf.co.uk;
info@aappl.com; www.aappl.com

Sales and Distribution
UK and export: Turnaround Publisher Services Ltd.
orders@turnaround-uk.com
USA and Canada: Sterling Publishing Inc. sales@sterlingpub.com
Australia & New Zealand: Peribo Pty. peribomec@bigpond.com
South Africa: Trinity Books. trinity@iafrica.com

A catalogue record for this book is available from the British
Library.

ISBN 1-904332-22-6

Design (contents and cover): Malcolm Couch
mal.couch@blueyonder.co.uk

Printed in China by Imago Publishing
info@imago.co.uk

CONTENTS

THE GAME OF TENNIS 7

The Name 7

The Game 7

Real Tennis 7

Lawn Tennis 13

The Other Championships 20

THE CLUB 22

THE CHAMPIONSHIPS 27

Background 27

Prize Money 31

Men's Singles 35

Men's Doubles 38

Some Facts about the Men 42

Ladies' Singles 49

Ladies' Doubles 52

Some facts about the Ladies 55

Mixed Doubles 64

Grand Slam Winners 67

The Championships Today 69

WIMBLEDON 79

The Place 79

The Buildings 80

Transport 90

The Common 91

The Windmill 94

THE GAME OF TENNIS

—— THE NAME ——

The word *tennis* (old French *tenes*) derives from the equivalent of the modern French term *tenez*, imperative of the verb *tenir* (to hold). In middle English the word variously appears as *tenetz, teneys, tenes, tenyse*.

There is an Egyptian town on the Nile called Tinnis (in Arabic) and some believe the game may have its roots here.

—— THE GAME ——
REAL TENNIS

The game started to form into something recognisable in the 12th and 13th Centuries. It began as hand ball, played by monks around the cloisters of monasteries in Italy and France. In time they took to wearing gloves and later using a bat, or racket.

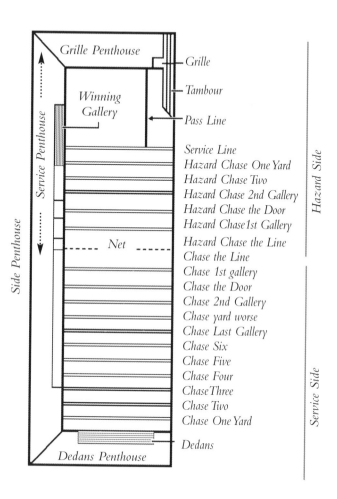

Layout of a Real Tennis court

Tennis in the UK was originally played in a walled court. This version of the sport, known nowadays as Real (ie: Royal) Tennis was popularised in England in the 15th and 16th Centuries, particularly at court during the reign of Henry VIII and the game has hardly changed since then.

Real Tennis today is called Royal Tennis in Australia, Court Tennis in the States and Jeu de Paume ("handball") in France.

As it is the oldest of all the racket games some players in the UK believe it should be known properly as *Tennis*, the other, modern, game being *Lawn Tennis*.

Henry VIII was an addicted gambler and many of his financial problems were due to his massive wagers on the Real Tennis court.

Legend has it that Henry VIII heard of the execution of his Queen, Anne Boleyn, as he played tennis at Hampton Court Palace.

Henry VIII had a servant to throw the ball up in the air for him because he was too fat to do it himself. There is an entry in Hampton Court's accounts in 1531 recording the payment of five shillings (45 cents) to "one that served on the King's side at Tennes", hence the word "service".

Charles I built a court at Hampton Court (about 6 miles from Wimbledon) in 1625 which is still used for championship play today. Visitors to Hampton Court Palace can visit the

Real Tennis court. Many later kings and other members of the royal family have been Real Tennis players. There is a locker in the changing room at Hampton Court Palace which still bears the name of Prince Albert (1819-1861).

The Archbishop of Rouen in 1245 prohibited his priests from engaging in "handball". King Louis IX also outlawed the sport. Such prohibitions carried over to England, where the game was outlawed in 1388 because the people were failing to practice archery

Two kings lost their lives as a result of tennis: King Louis X of France (1314-16) and Charles VIII of France (1483-98). It is said that Louis X died of a chill immediately after playing an energetic game of *jeu de paume* at Château de Vincennes. Charles VIII died after striking his head on a horizontal piece of wood over the door which led to his tennis court.

The 1599 French rules allowed for an on-the-spot fine of 5 sous for swearing on court.

The court at Versailles (Paris) was built in 1686 at a cost then of 45,403 Francs (about £4,000 or $7,500). In the 17th Century during the game's heyday there were as many as 1800 courts in Paris alone.

A court was built in a palace in St. Petersburg, Russia in the 1790's. It is now a gym but there are plans to convert it back into a Real Tennis court.

The first courts in the USA were built in 1876, and in Australia in 1882.

No two Real Tennis courts are exactly alike. That at Hampton Court is marginally wider than all others in England. Other differences include the width or angle of the penthouse roof above the corridor which runs around three sides of the court. Each court is about 110 feet (33 metres) long, 40 feet (12 metres) wide and 30 feet (9 metres) high; the net is 5 feet (1.5 metres) high at the ends but sags to 3 feet (under 1 metre) in the middle.

Today there are approximately 6 active courts in Australia (with new courts planned), 3 in France, 27 in the UK and 10 in the USA (with further courts being planned).

Early balls were made of leather stuffed with wool or human hair and could be hard enough to cause injury to players struck by a ball moving at speed. In the 15th Century balls were generally white, to show up against the black walls. In Spain it was the other way round. The modern ball is similar in appearance to a lawn tennis ball but is made with a core of cork, covered in cloth, tightly bound in string and finally covered in felt.

In Henry VIII's time balls cost 1 penny each and manufacture and sale of the balls was controlled, for some reason, by the Ironmonger's Guild. The UK public records have a 1599 entry noting the import from "the Continent of tennys balles for £1,699 ($ 3,000)".

Originally the game was played with the bare hand, later with a glove. The term *racquet* or *racket* is thought to derive from the Arabic word *rahat* which means *the palm of the hand*.

Rackets were originally small "paddles" of solid wood. By 1500 they were no longer completely made of wood but consisted of a wooden handle with a sheep gut strung head.

Racket heads were asymetrical to allow the player to scoop up the ball from the corner of the court in the angle of the walls.

The Rules state: racket frames… shall be made almost entirely of wood, but may include essential laminates made of other materials.

Grays of Cambridge are the only Real Tennis racket makers left in the UK.

RULES INCLUDE:

*Players shall conduct themselves, both on and off
the Court, in a manner consistent with the etiquette,
sportsmanship and exemplary standards of behaviour
and dress expected of the sport.
Players shall accept success, failure, victory or defeat with
good grace and without excessive display of emotion…*

LAWN TENNIS

In 1858, Major T.H. Gem and J.B. Perara invented an outdoor version of Real Tennis adapted for play on grass and called it Pelota, after the Spanish game.

SPHAIRISTIKE

Lawn Tennis was invented in about 1873,
as a game to be played on a marked-out surface
without side or end walls (unlike Real Tennis)
by Major Walter Clipton Wingfield.
who originally called it 'Sphairistike', the name of an
ancient Greek ball game.
This was sometimes abbreviated to "sticky"
although it was not the name that stuck.
The term *Lawn Tennis* was probably coined by
Arthur Balfour, a British Statesman and very early
player of Sphairistike, though Major Gem also
laid some claim to having created the term.

The shape of the Sphairistike court was an "hourglass", narrower at the net than at the ends.

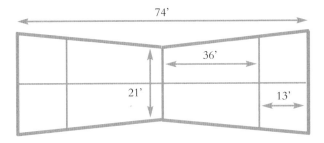

Some contemporary press comment:-

" it is a clever adaptation of tennis [Real Tennis]… what more acceptable present for the Easter holidays "

The Court Journal

"…new game…will become a national pastime."

Army and Navy Gazette

"The game has much more healthy and manly excitement than croquet…it should be hailed as a public boon, even at Dundee, where it should not be forgotten that all work and no play is a bad thing."

Dundee Advertiser

"It is a barbarious name…why a less jaw-breaking name could not have been found is a question which I leave you to settle with the inventor…there was a great run on the game in France as soon as it was discovered that it might be played without the necessity of pronouncing it…it comes in a box no bigger than a double gun-case"

Sporting Gazette

"eminently social, sociable and comfortable"

The Globe

" a game at which ladies can display considerable proficiency"

Morning Post

"The monopoly of croquet is at last broken."

Daily Telegraph

"The server has rather too great an advantage since a clean-cut ball, passing just over the net into the farthest corner of the opposite court, is all but impossible to return."

Vanity Fair

Wingfield's 1873 book *The Game of Sphairistike* (written in Greek letters!) *or Lawn Tennis* stated:
" the merest tyro can learn it in 5 minutes sufficiently well for all practical purposes
… in a hard frost the net may be erected on the ice and, the players being equipped with skates, the game assumes a new feature…"

In his book Wingfield listed some of the people who had already bought a set of Sphairistike. They included 10 princes and princesses, 7 dukes, 14 marquises, 1 marchioness, 1 governor-general (of Canada), 49 earls, 10 countesses, 8 viscounts and page upon page of lords, ladies, knights and baronets, honourables and right honourables.

The first boxed sets cost 5 guineas (£5.25p / $9.50) and comprised a net and posts, 4 bats [sic], balls, mallett, line-brush and a book of rules. Loose rubber balls were 5 shillings (25p /45cents) per dozen, kid-covered 10 shillings.

Arguably it was the 'portability' of the Sphairistike equipment set that was responsible for the game's speedy introduction (probably by Mary Outerbridge) to the USA, in 1874. She obtained a Sphairistike set while on holiday in Bermuda and took it back to her Staten Island home, though there is still some argument as to exactly when this happened.

In the year of 1874 sets were exported to USA, Canada, Germany, France, Switzerland, South Africa, China, India, Greece and Russia. There are thought to be around 750,000 tennis courts around the world today.

The first recorded death on a tennis court was one Colonel Osborne at the Hyde Park Tennis Club, London, in the 1880's.

India rubber was first used in the core of tennis balls from the 1870's and still is today. Each year around 300 million premium-quality tennis balls are sold around the world. In real terms (ie allowing for inflation) tennis balls today cost about 20% of what they cost in the 1920s in USA but in UK around 80%. Balls in UK cost over double the current US price.

A wooden racket was last used at Wimbledon in 1987 and 1981 was the last year in which both men's finalists (Borg & McEnroe) used wooden rackets. Today rackets are generally made of carbon fibre reinforced with graphite, kevlar and titanium. The modern racket weighs 210-280 g (7-10 oz) compared with the last wooden rackets at 370-425 g (13-15 oz). The head size is 25% bigger nowadays.

The original lawn tennis rackets were strung with the intestines of pigs, horses and sheep. Although various synthetic materials have been tried since, most professionals still prefer rackets to be strung with gut. It takes the "contents" of between 3 and 5 sheep, or about 12 metres (40 feet) of gut to string one racket. Cow gut can also be used.

Top-quality tennis shoes today are made with leather uppers and polyurethane soles.

The rules of tennis were originally administered by the MCC (Marylebone Cricket Club), based at the Lords cricket ground in central London.

Wimbledon took over the administration of the rules in 1877 abandoning the hourglass court shape and standardising the new courts at 78 x 27 feet (23.75 x 8.2 metres). The rules have remained unchanged in any significant fashion ever since, with the exception of the tie break introduced in 1970s.

The mysterious scoring system extends back at least as far the early 15th Century since it is mentioned in a poem about the Battle of Agincourt written by Charles D'Orlean in 1435.

How the Point Scoring Works:

When either player wins his first point in any game,
his score is called fifteen;
when he wins his second point, thirty,
when he wins his third point, forty
and when he wins his fourth point, he wins the game
except that when both players have won three points,
the score is called *deuce* and it is called *advantage*
to the player who wins the next point.
If the player who is at advantage wins the next
point, he wins the game.
If he loses it, the score is again called *deuce*
and so on until the player who is at advantage
wins a point and the game.

THE VOCABULARY OF TENNIS

JM Barrie, author of *Peter Pan,* once commented:
"What a polite game tennis is; the chief word seems to be "sorry"!".

Ace: a good serve untouched by the opponent.
Alley: the area between the singles and doubles line.
Backcourt: the back half of the court between the service and baselines.
Break: when the player serving loses the game.
Clay Court: a court with a crushed brick or stone surface.
Deuce: a tie at 40 points.
Double Fault: two service faults in a row.
Dropshot: a sliced, spinning shot which stops quickly with little bounce.
Fault: when the ball is hit into the net.
Foot Fault: the server steps onto or over the baseline before hitting the ball.
Game point: the point required to win a game.
Groundstroke: a shot played after the ball has bounced.
Half Volley: shot played immediately after the ball has bounced.
Hard court: a court with an asphalt or concrete surface.
Let: called when an otherwise good serve touches the net and the point is replayed.
Lob: A high shot with the ball intended to land behind the opponent.
Love: zero points.
Match: a series of 3 or 5 sets.
Passing shot: a shot played when the opponent is close to the net and cannot reach the ball.

Rally: a long exchange of shots.
Tie-breaker: when the players tie at 6 games each
a deciding game is played, the winner being the
first player to reach minimum 7 points with a
minimum 2 points lead.
Unforced error: a point lost by a player under
no apparent pressure from his opponent
Volley: the return of the ball before it bounces.

The word *deuce* is derived from the French "a deux du jeu" -
two points away from game, the English having shortened it
first to "a deus" ("deus" being "deux" in old French) and
thence to *deuce*.

The term *love* meaning "no points" may come from the
Dutch language. Around the time that the expression came
to be used, there were a large number of refugees coming
to England from the low countries, driven away by the
incoming Protestantism. Bearing in mind that most games
were played for money, if a player scored no points, the phrase
"omme lof spelen" would have been applicable - "playing for
the honour". Some people believe *love* comes from the
French word "l'oeuf" meaning "the egg", though it is not
clear quite why this should be...
"*In a sport where love means nothing it's not surprising that etiquette
means everything.*" New York Times, 1978.

Umpire comes from old French (as do so many English
words). The term *noumpere* in 14th Century French referred
to an independent person brought in to settle a dispute. The
word was wrongly divided in later English when instead of
referring to *a noumpere* or *a nounpier*, popular usage turned it
into *an ounpier*, now *an umpire*.

THE OTHER
COMPETITIONS

The US Lawn Tennis Association was formed in 1881 but the first championship competition took place the previous year at the Staten Island Cricket and Baseball Club. The first National Championship, precursor to the **US Open** of today, was held in 1881. Until 1974 it was played on grass, switching then to clay courts, but changing again in 1978 to hard court. Jimmy Connors won on all 3 surfaces.

The first **French Open** took place in 1891 and was played on grass. Women were first invited in 1897 and it was opened to non-French players in 1925. The French Open tends to be known today after the stadium where it is played, "Roland Garros". Yannick Noah was the last Frenchman to win there, in 1983.

In 1896 men's singles and doubles play was included on the programme for the first modern **Olympic Games**.

The International Lawn Tennis Challenge Trophy, known as the **Davis Cup**, was first contested in 1900. It is now the top international team competition and is for men only. An American tennis player Dwight Davis, a doubles specialist, donated the Davis cup to the tennis community and the cup itself is officially (but never in reality…) called "The International Lawn Tennis Challenge Trophy". The Davis Cup has been won by UK, USA, France, Australia, South Africa, Sweden, Italy, Czecholslovakia, Germany, Russia and Spain. Around 140 nations now enter the competition. The women's equivalent, though not as well-known, is the **Fed Cup**, founded in 1963 as The Federation Cup. Around 100 countries now take part.

The **Australian Open**, then called the Australian National Championship, had its debut in 1905. Women were first admitted in 1922. The championships take place in Melbourne. Until 1988 they were on grass but are now on a rubberised hard court. This was the first Open to have commercial sponsorship; from 1974-84 from Marlboro cigarettes and from 1985-97 from Ford.

The **Wightman Cup**, a competition between British and American women's teams, started in 1923 and came to an end in 1989.

A player who wins the 4 main championships (Wimbledon, US, Australia and France) is said to have won the **Grand Slam**. This is bridge (cards) terminology and was used in respect of tennis for the first time in 1938 by Allison Danzig, writing in the New York Times, describing Donald Budge's achievement as the first person to win all 4 titles in one calendar year. Maureen Connolly was the first woman to achieve this, in 1953. Confusingly a player winning one of these tournaments is spoken of as winning *a* (not *the*) Grand Slam or simply "a slam".

The International Lawn Tennis Federation, the **ITF**, was founded in 1913 to try to develop a uniform approach to the game's rules and assist its general development around the world. It is now the world governing body for tennis.

Professional tennis started in 1926 when the French star Suzanne Lenglen was paid US$50,000 (£28,000) for a tour. Professionalism received full worldwide acceptance in 1968 when professionals were first allowed to compete at Wimbledon. The main worldwide competitions today offer over $100,000,000 in prize money each year. Pete Sampras has earned over $40,000,000 in prize money and Steffi Graf over $21,000,000 in addition to their massive earnings from sponsorship and so on.

Ladies playing croquet, 1870

THE CLUB

The All England Lawn Tennis and Croquet Club was founded in 1868. It was originally a croquet club and called *The All England Croquet Club*. It took on its present name in the spring of 1877 and held the first lawn tennis championships that year to raise money for a pony-drawn roller for its croquet lawns. In 1882 the club stopped offering croquet to its members and dropped reference to this sport from its name. It was restored to the name in 1899, probably for sentimental reasons, and has stuck ever since. The name is often shortened to *AELTC*.

The club was founded by John Walsh, editor of *The Field* magazine, together with 5 friends. The first year's rent for the 4 acre (1.66 hectares) site was £50 (US$90). The club had 12 croquet lawns and held its first competition in 1870.

Croquet is played at the present location. The croquet lawn was laid in 1957 but it is not full size so is only used for Club tournaments.

The *AELTC* is still a private club with only some 375 full members plus a number of honorary members. The latter include past singles champions, of various nationalities. There are also about 100 temporary members, who are elected from year to year. The reason for the small number of members is that each of them has the right to purchase two tickets for each day of the championships and if the membership were increased it would reduce the number of tickets available to the public.

The *AELTC*'s first ground was situated off Worple Road, Wimbledon. In 1922 the club moved to the present site in Church Road. The new ground was opened by King George V.

The club colors, dark green and purple, were introduced in 1909. No-one seems to know why this combination was chosen.

In 1913 suffragettes tried to burn down the old Centre Court stand but were caught in the act.

The grounds themseves are owned by a company called The All England Lawn Tennis Ground plc, which is owned equally by the *AELTC* and The Lawn Tennis Association.

The club grounds contain 19 grass courts, five red shale, three clay and five indoor courts. There are 22 grass courts for practice before and during the Championships and two acrylic courts. The courts are used all year round by the club members and LTA-sponsored players (except for centre and No.1 courts). The grass courts can be used from May to September. Centre Court and No.1 court are used only for the championships

Centre Court, built in 1922, is so named because at the original Worple Road venue the main court was literally built in the centre, surrounded by the "lesser" courts. The name was preserved at the new site although it was no longer an accurate description of the court's location. When additional courts were built in 1980 Centre Court ended up pretty much in the middle once again.

Above the players' entrance to Centre Court is the quotation from Kipling's *If*: *"If you can meet with triumph and disaster and treat those two impostors just the same"*.

Until 1990 Centre Court had places for 2000 standing spectators; it is now all-seating.

Money to maintain the grounds and their facilities is raised through the sale, every 5 years, of debentures. These allow the debenture holder to buy one ticket for Centre Court for each day of play for 5 years. There are 2,300 debentures in issue. One debenture for 2006 – 2010 cost £23,150 (US$ 40,500) or £1,780 (US$ 3,120) *per day*. The last debentures on offer sold out immediately. Debenture holders do get their own dining-room…

Club members and their guests (male) have to wear jacket and tie in the members' enclosure (a posh tea-tent). Ladies may wear "smart trouser suits" but jeans or shorts are not acceptable. Unlike members using the catering facilities of the members' enclosure, debenture holders (male and female) using the debenture-holders' lounge may wear "smart shorts".

Wimbledon is justifiably proud of the standard of its courts. In 1886 " *an industrious and forceful player observed the presence of a daisy on Centre Court and in consequence missed otherwise certain victory.*" The reason why no play takes place in the mornings is partly to allow the ground-staff time to repair and maintain the playing surfaces.

The permanent members of staff are:
Office: chief executive, championships director, finance director, marketing director, director of TV rights, IT director, club secretary. There are about 40 other administrative staff.

Ground Staff: Head groundsman, 14–15 other ground staff and a team of 32 maintenance staff.

Other staff: There are 4 full-time dressing-rooms staff and 12–14 full and part-time in the members' dining room.

Over 6,000 people now work at or for Wimbledon fortnight. These include a temporary staff of several hundred who are directly employed by the AELTC.

During the Second World War the club remained open and the buildings were used for civil defence and military functions including fire and ambulance services, Home Guard and a decontamination unit. Troops stationed in the area were allowed to use the main concourse for drilling. In October 1940 five 500lb German bombs struck Centre Court, resulting in the loss of 1,200 seats but no lives.

The club's official website www.wimbledon.org receives over 240 million page views and 4.3 million unique visitors each year.

THE CHAMPIONSHIPS

—————— Background ——————

Wimbledon is the only Grand Slam to be played on grass.

The first championships took place in 1877 and the only event was the men's singles. The first winner of the title was Mr Spencer Gore, aged 37, an Englishman educated at Harrow School. Gore won the match in only fifty minutes and reportedly said afterwards "Lawn Tennis is a bit boring. It will never catch on."

Each of the 22 competitors in 1877 paid an entry fee of one guinea (£1.05 / US$1.90).

At the first championships there were no stands. Spectators stood on the sidelines or sat in their carriages.

The winner of the first men's singles title would receive a trophy valued at 25 guineas (£26.25 or US$ 48), presented by *The Field*, a magazine, which played a major role in the early development of the sport. The 2004 men's champion won £602,500 ($1.1 million).

The first set of rules included: "players must wear shoes without heels". They also wore a tie and hat.

At Wimbledon in 1877 serves were played underarm.

In 1890 all 3 titles (men's and ladies' singles and men's doubles) were won by Irish nationals.

Norman Brookes of Australia was the first non-UK/Ireland winner, in 1907.

Until 1922 the reigning champion only had to play in the final, against whoever had won through to challenge him.

At the first championships to be played at Church Rd, in 1922, it rained every day and play did not finish until the Wednesday of week three.

Since the championship moved to Church Rd in 1922 only two players from Great Britain, Arthur Gore and Fred Perry, have managed to win the men's singles.

In the years from 1934 to 1937, the golden era for British tennis, a total of 11 titles were won, including three successive singles by Fred Perry and two by Dorothy Round. During the same period Great Britain successfully defended the Davis Cup three times in competitions staged on Centre Court.

The years just before the Second World War belonged to the United States. Donald Budge won all three events in 1937 and 1938 and Helen Wills Moody won the ladies' singles eight times.

In 1939 when the Second World War began, the championships were suspended until 1946

1968 was the year of the first "open" or professional championships; the prize money was £2,000 for the men's and £750 for the women's singles champion. (US$3,500 / $1,400).

Players from over 60 nations now compete at Wimbledon.

In 1877 200 people watched the men's singles final. In 2004 the number at Centre Court was 14,000.

The maximum capacity of the ground is currently 35,500.

"Strawberries, cream and champers flowed like hot cakes." –
Radio 2

Over the 5 years to 2004 total attendance for the championships was :

2000	455,752
2001	490,081
2002	469,514
2003	470,802
2004	451,208

The record attendance for the meeting is 490,081 in 2001, when play was extended into a 14th day. The record for the meeting, over the normal scheduled 13 days, is 476,711 also in 2001.

Record attendances for each day are as follows:

First week:

Monday 39,330 (2001)
Tuesday 41,929 (2003)
Wednesday 42,457 (2002)
Thursday 41,976 (2003)
Friday 41,595 (2002)
Saturday 40,043 (2001)
Sunday 31,204 (1997)

Second week:

Monday 41,236 (2001)
Tuesday 38,577 (1985)
Wednesday 36,969 (2001)
Thursday 33,560 (2002)
Friday 32,453 (1999)
Saturday 29,566 (1999)
Sunday 30,802 (1999)

Third Week:

Monday 15,257 (1988)

PRIZE MONEY
(2004)
($ amounts based on exchange rate of £1/$1.8)

Men's Singles
Winner   £602,500 / $1,084,500
Runner-Up   £301,250 / $542,250
Semi-Finalists   £150,630 / $271,000
Quarter-Finalists   £78,330 / $150,000
Losers of the 4th Round   £42,170 / $76,000
Losers of the 3rd Round   £24,390 / $44,000

Ladies' Singles
Winner   £560,390 / $1,010,000
Runner-Up   £280,250 / $505,000
Semi-Finalists   £135,560 / $244,000
Quarter-Finalists   £68,540 / $123,000
Losers of the 4th Round   £35,850 / $64,500
Losers of the 3rd Round   £19,510 / $35,000

Men's Doubles
Winner   £215,000 / $387,000
Runner-Up   £107,500 / $193,500
Semi-Finalists   £55,100/ $99,000
Quarter-Finalists   £28,600 / $51,500
Losers of the 3rd Round   £15,200/ $27,500
Losers of the 2nd Round   £8,300/ $15,000

Ladies' Doubles
Winner   £200,000/ $360,000
Runner-Up   £100,000 / $180,000
Semi-Finalists   £50,000 / $90,000
Quarter-Finalists   £25,000 / $45,000
Losers of the 3rd Round   £12,850 / $23,000
Losers of the 2nd Round   £6,600/ $12,000

Matches were first televised by the BBC in 1937 but it was not until after the Second World War that they were televised each day. The first colour television broadcast from Wimbledon came in 1967.

The modern championships receive more than 5,500 hours of worldwide coverage. It is believed that about 1.8 billion (1,800,000,000) people saw at least part of the 2004 championships. In the United Kingdom, the BBC transmits around 160 hours of coverage during the fortnight.

BBC Outside Broadcasts install some 66,700 metres, or 41 miles, of signal cable for the championships. In 2004 there were 54 cameras on site. The BBC hoist from which the aerial shots are taken is 72 metres tall (236 feet) and carries one manned camera and two robotic ones

In 1986 the championships adopted yellow tennis balls for the first time - partly to make the speeding balls more visible for television cameras.

More than 2,000 press passes are issued for the fortnight.

"I know where the press room is …where they throw the dog-meat"
Martina Navratilova

Some quotes from commentators:

"The Gullikson twins here. An interesting pair, both from Wisconsin"
Dan Maskell

"Ann's got to take her nerve by the horns"
Virgina Wade

"Martina, she's got several layers of steel out there like a cat with nine lives"
Viginia Wade

"Strangely enough, Kathy Jordan is getting to the net first, which she always does"
Fred Perry

"Lloyd did what he achieved with that shot"
Jack Bannister

"He's got his hands on his knees and holds his head in despair"
Peter Jones

"Chip Hooper is such a big man that it is sometimes difficult to see where he is on the court"
Mark Cox

"Lendl has remained throughout as calm as the proverbial iceberg"
Dan Maskell

"This is the third week the fish seem to be getting away from British tennis players"
Gerald Williams

The tournament starts each year six weeks before the first Monday in August and lasts for two weeks (*Wimbledon Fortnight*) or for as long as necessary to complete all events. In the 5 years to 2004 only 2 days were completely rained off, both in the first week in 2004. In 1922 it rained every day.

> *"We haven't had any more rain since it stopped raining"*
> Harry Carpenter

Play normally starts on Centre and No. 1 courts at 1.00 p.m. for the first eleven days and at 2.00 p.m. on finals days. On all other courts the start of play is 12.00 noon for at least the first eight days and 11.00 a.m. for junior matches on the middle Saturday and during the second week.

At the first championships a ticket to the finals cost 1 shilling (5 pence/9 cents). In 2004 it cost £73 to £79 (approx US$130-US$140) but tickets are known to have changed hands at well over £1,000 (US$ 1,800) each on the unofficial market. Corporate hospitality days, including Centre Court seat, food and wine, are on offer from around £2,000 ($3,800) per person for the day of the men's finals.

Applications for tickets in the first year at Church Rd (1922) were such that they had to be issued by a ballot – a system that has been adopted for every championship since.

A member of the British royal family has presented the trophy to every men's singles champion at Wimbledon since the war, except in 1986 when Boris Becker received his trophy from the French Davis Cup legend Jean Borotra

MEN'S SINGLES CHAMPIONS

1877	Spencer Gore
1878	Frank Hadow
1879–1880	John Hartley
1881–1886	William Renshaw
1887	Herbert Lawford
1888	Ernest Renshaw
1889	William Renshaw
1890	William Hamilton
1891–1892	Wifred Baddeley
1893–1894	Joshua Pim
1895	Wilfred Baddeley
1896	Harold Mahoney
1897–1900	Reggie Doherty
1901	Arthur Gore
1902–1906	Laurie Doherty
1907	Norman Brookes
1908–1909	Arthur Gore
1910–1913	A. F. Wilding
1914	N. E. Brookes
1919	G. L. Patterson
1920–1921	Bill Tilden
1922	G. L. Patterson
1923	William Johnston
1924	Jean Borotra
1925	Rene Lacoste
1926	Jean Borotra
1927	Henri Cochet
1928	Rene Lacoste
1929	Jean Cochet
1930	Bill Tilden
1931	S. B. Wood

1932	Ellsworth Vines
1933	J. H. Crawford
1934–1936	Fred Perry
1937–1938	Don Budge
1939	Bobby Riggs
1946	Yvon Petra
1947	Jack Kramer
1948	R. Falkenburg
1949	Fred Schroeder
1950	Budge Patty
1951	Richard Savitt
1952	Frank Sedgman
1953	Vic Siexas
1954	Jaroslav Drobny
1955	Tony Trabert
1956–1957	Lewis Hoad
1958	Ashley Cooper
1959	Alex Olmedo
1960	Neale Fraser
1961–1962	Rod Laver
1963	Chuck McKinley
1964–1965	Roy Emerson
1966	Manuel Santana
1967	John Newcombe
1968–1969	Rod Laver
1970–1971	John Newcombe
1972	Stan Smith
1973	Jan Kodes
1974	Jimmy Connors
1975	Arthur Ashe
1976–1980	Bjorn Borg
1981	John McEnroe

1982	Jimmy Connors
1983-1984	John McEnroe
1985-1986	Boris Becker
1987	Pat Cash
1988	Stefan Edberg
1989	Boris Becker
1990	Stefan Edberg
1991	Michael Stich
1992	Andre Agassi
1993-1995	Pete Sampras
1996	Richard Krajicek
1997-2000	Pete Sampras
2001	Goran Ivanisevic
2002	Lleyton Hewitt
2003-2004	Roger Federer
2005	....
2006	....
2007	....
2008	....

"Those two volleys really could be the story of this match summed up at the end of it"
Barry Davies

"New Yorkers love it when you spill your guts out there. Spill your guts at Wimbledon and they make you stop and clean it up".
Jimmy Connors

The men's winner receives a silver gilt cup made in 1887. This is kept on display at the Wimbledon Tennis Museum.

The men's singles have been won by the following nationalities:

United States (33),
British Isles (formerly used to designate
UK & Republic of Ireland) (32),
Australia (21),
France (7),
Sweden (7),
Germany (4),
New Zealand (4),
Britain (3),
Switzerland (2)
Czechoslovakia (1),
Egypt (1),
Netherlands (1),
Spain (1).
Croatia (1)

Men's Doubles Champions

Gentlemen's Doubles was started in 1884 and the winners' trophy was donated by Oxford University Lawn Tennis Club who had themselves hosted national doubles championships from 1879 to 1883.

1884–1886	William Renshaw/Ernest Renshaw
1887	Herbert Wilberforce/P.B. Lyon
1888–1889	William Renshaw/Ernest Renshaw
1890	Joshua Pim/F.O. Stoker
1891	Wilfred Baddeley/Herbert Baddeley
1892	E.W. Lewis/H.S. Barlow
1893	Joshua Pim/F.O. Stoker
1894–1896	Wilfred Baddeley/Herbert Baddeley
1897–1901	Reggie Doherty/Laurie Doherty
1902	Sidney Smith/Frank Riseley
1903–1905	Reggie Doherty/Laurie Doherty
1906	Sidney Smith/Frank Riseley
1907	Norman Brookes/Tony Wilding
1908	Tony Wilding/Josiah Ritchie
1909	Arthur Gore/H. Roper Barrett
1910	Tony Wilding/Josiah Ritchie
1911	Andre Gobert/Max Decugis
1912–1913	H. Roper Barrett/Charles Dixon
1914	Norman Brookes/Tony Wilding
1915–1918	*not played*
1919	R.V. Thomas/Pat O'Hara Wood
1920	Richard Williams/Chuck Garland
1921	Randolph Lycett/Max Woosnam
1922	James Anderson/Randolph Lycett
1923	Leslie Godfree/Randolph Lycett
1924	Frank Hunter/Vincent Richards

1925	Jean Borotra/Rene Lacoste
1926	Jacques Brugnon/Henri Cochet
1927	Frank Hunter/Bill Tilden
1928	Jacques Brugnon/Henri Cochet
1929-1930	Wilmer Allison/John Van Ryn
1931	George Lott/John Van Ryn
1932-1933	Jean Borotra/Jacques Brugnon
1934	George Lott/Lester Stoefen
1935	Jack Crawford/Adrian Quist
1936	G. Pat Hughes/Raymond Tuckey
1937-1938	Don Budge/Gene Mako
1939	Elwood Cooke/Bobby Riggs
1940-1945	*not played*
1946	Tom Brown/Jack Kramer
1947	Bob Falkenburg/Jack Kramer
1948	John Bromwich/Frank Sedgman
1949	Richard Gonzales/Frank Parker
1950	John Bromwich/Adrian Quist
1951-1952	Ken McGregor/Frank Sedgman
1953	K. Rosewall/L. Hoad
1954	R. Hartwig/M. Rose
1955	R. Hartwig/L. Hoad
1956	L. Hoad/K. Rosewall
1957	Gardnar Mulloy/Budge Patty
1958	Sven Davidson/Ulf Schmidt
1959	Roy Emerson/Neale Fraser
1960	Dennis Ralston/Rafael Osuna
1961	Roy EmersonNeale Fraser
1962	Fred Stolle/Bob Hewitt
1963	Rafael Osuna/Antonio Palafox
1964	Fred Stolle/Bob Hewitt
1965	John Newcombe/Tony Roche
1966	John Newcombe/Ken Fletcher

1967	Bob Hewitt/Frew McMillan
1968–1970	John Newcombe/Tony Roche
1971	Rod Laver/Roy Emerson
1972	Bob Hewitt/Frew McMillan
1973	Jimmy Connors/Ilie Nastase
1974	John Newcombe/Tony Roche
1975	Vitas Gerulaitis/Sandy Mayer
1976	Brian Gottfried/Raul Ramirez
1977	Ross Case/Geoff Masters
1978	Fred McMillan/Bob Hewitt
1979	Peter Fleming/John McEnroe
1980	Peter McNamara/Paul McNamee
1981	John McEnroe/Peter Fleming
1982	Paul McNamee/Peter McNamara
1983-1984	John McEnroe/Peter Fleming
1985	Heinz Gunthardt/Balazs Taroczy
1986	Joakim Nystrom/Mats Wilander
1987–1988	Ken Flach/Robert Seguso
1989	John Fitzgerald/Anders Jarryd
1990	Rick Leach/Jim Pugh
1991	Anders Jarryd/John Fitzgerald
1992	John McEnroeMichael Stich
1993-1997	Todd Woodbridge/Mark Woodforde
1998	Jacco Eltingh/Paul Haarhuis
1999	Mahesh Bhupathi/Leander Paes
2000	Todd Woodbridge/Mark Woodforde
2001	Donald Johnson/Jared Palmer
2002–2004	Todd Woodbridge/Jonas Bjorkman
2005	....
2006	....
2007	....
2008	....

SOME FACTS
ABOUT THE MEN

In 1879 the Rev. J.T. Hartley, who drove home halfway through the tournament to give a sermon, defeated Vere Thomas St. Leger Goold in the final. Goold and his wife were later convicted in France for dismembering a woman's body and he was sent to prison on Devil's Island, where he eventually died.

The Renshaw twins, who dominated Wimbledon in the 1880s, were the first to use the overarm service.

Arthur Gore played at Wimbledon in 1888 and at every subsequent Wimbledon until 1927, a total of 35 championships. He is the oldest player to win the singles (41), the oldest finalist (44); he won Olympic Gold in singles and doubles in 1908 and captained Great Britain in the inaugural Davis Cup in 1900.

In 1907 Norman Brookes, an Australian, became the first men's singles champion from overseas. He was also the first left-hander to win Wimbledon. He became Sir Norman Brookes in 1939.

William Tatem Tilden II, a.k.a. "Big Bill" was one of the great stars of the 1920's. Tilden's unique style of play featured booming serves and long strides across the court that enabled him to stay back near the baseline. Seven times he won the United States Championship. Eleven times he was a Davis Cup team member. Tilden was the first American to triumph at Wimbledon in 1920. When he finally retired, he had won over 70 tennis championships and earned his nick-name – "king of the nets."

Randolph Lycett arrived on Centre Court in 1921 with a trainer carrying a bottle of champagne for the player. He lost.

In the 1920's Frenchman Jean Borotra was known as "the bounding Basque" because of his habit of leaping into the stands to doff his beret to whichever pretty girl caught his eye. Compliment paid, he would jump back and resume play. Borotra and fellow-countrymen Brugnon, Cochet and Lacoste, known as "the 4 musketeers", won 6 Wimbledon men's singles and 5 doubles titles between them during the 1920's. Borotra was Minister for Sport in France from 1940-42, when he was arrested by the German occupying forces. Renee Lacoste's nickname was "the crocodile" and this became the logo on his Lacoste clothing range.

Australian Gerald Patterson was the first returning champion to have to play through the whole competition after the rule-change in 1922, which did away with the challenge round, which had permitted the returning champion just to play in the final match. Patterson won the title.

Bunny Austin was the first man ever to wear a pair of shorts on court at Wimbledon in 1933.

American Bobby Riggs won the singles, doubles and mixed doubles on his first visit to Wimbledon in 1939. At age 55 he stated publicly that no woman tennis player could beat a man and he challenged Billie Jean King and lost. He said " *I'll put the women's libbers back where they belong – in the kitchen and the bedroom.* "

○

Fred Perry was a table tennis champion before starting to play lawn tennis at age 18. He became the first player to win all 4 Grand Slam titles. Don Budge was the first to win them all in one year and he played professionally until age 55.

○

There were few multiple title-winners in the 1940s and 50s because in those days any winner, then all amateurs, was immediately approached to turn professional and they were thus disqualified from defending their Wimbledon title.

○

Yvon Petra was the last champion to wear long trousers on court in 1946.

○

Thomas Lejus, of Estonia, who won the Wimbledon boys' singles title in 1959, representing the Soviet Union, later spent five years in jail for the manslaughter of his wife.

○

Rod Laver was the only person to win the calendar year Grand Slam twice, in 1962 and 1969, the first as an amateur, the second as a professional. He played left-handed.

○

Manolo Santana (Spain) preferred to play on clay and after winning Wimbledon in 1966 commented "*Grass is for cows*".

○

Australian Tony Roche won 3 Wimbledon titles in 1968, 69

and 70 and then suffered severe elbow problems which he dealt with successfully by having an anaesthetic-free operation in the Phillippines.

Arthur Ashe was the first black man to win a Grand Slam tournament.

In 1974, during a heated argument with the umpire Ilie Nastase was heard to say "You call me *Mr* Nastase!" Since then all umpires use this form of address when giving a player a warning.

Bjorn Borg was the first player at the Church Rd ground to win the men's singles 5 times in succession. He won 11 Grand Slam championships, a record beaten only by Pete Sampras (14 times) and Roy Emerson (12). He was also the first player to sign a significant sponsorship contract, with a men's clothing company (Fila).

Ivan Lendl won 8 Grand Slam titles between 1984 and 1990 but, despite reaching 2 finals and 5 semis, he never won Wimbledon. He holds the records for the most Grand Slam finals appearances, 19, and the most finals lost, 11 in all.

Swede Mats Wilander never won Wimbledon but was the first unseeded player to win at Roland Garros (the French Open), in 1982. He won 7 Grand Slam titles in all.

Jimmy Connors won the most singles titles with a total of 109. He reached the US Open semi-finals in 1991 at age 39.

John McEnroe uttered his famous "You can *not* be serious!" for the first time in 1981. He went on to win the match and the tournament. He won 77 singles and 77 doubles titles.

In 1985 Boris Becker became the youngest winner ever of the men's singles (he was 17 years, 227 days old), the 1st German and the 1st unseeded player to win at Wimbledon.

"The Woodies", Todd Woodbridge and Mark Woodforde won a record 5 doubles titles in consecutive years at Wimbledon from 1993-1997 and won the gold medal for Australia in the 1996 Olympics.

Andre Agassi is the son of a boxer who represented Iran in the 1952 Olympics.

In 1996, just as Richard Krajicek and Mali Vai Washington were about to begin play in the men's final, a 23 year old girl wearing only a small apron distracted them by streaking on Centre Court.

In 2003 Rod Laver and fellow Aussie Margaret Smith Court's portraits were used on Autralian postage stamps, a first for the sport.

Rod Laver was the first person to earn more than $1,000,000 from tennis. Pete Sampras is believed to have earned in excess of $40 million (£22.5 million) in prize money. Pete Sampras shares a record with Bjorn Borg with 8 consecutive years of winning at least one Grand Slam title.

Men's Wimbledon Records

Most men's singles: William Renshaw, **7** (1881-86, 1889).
Pete Sampras, **7** (1993-95, 1997-2000)
Most Men's Doubles: Laurie Doherty, **8** (1897-1901,
1903-05) Reggie Doherty, **8** (1897-1901, 1903-05)
Most Mixed Doubles Titles: Owen Davidson, **4** (1967, 1971,
1973-74) Ken Fletcher, **4** (1963, 1965-66, 1968)
Vic Seixas, **4** (1953-56)
Most Singles, Doubles, and Mixed Doubles Titles:
Laurie Doherty, **13** (5 singles, 8 doubles, 1897-1905)
Youngest Men's Singles Champion:
Boris Becker, 17 years, 227 days (1985)
Youngest Men's Doubles Champion:
Dennis Ralston, 17 years, 341 days (1960)
Youngest Mixed Doubles Champion:
Rod Laver, 20 years, 328 days (1959)
Oldest Men's Singles Champion:
Arthur Gore, 41 years, 182 days (1909)
Oldest Men's Doubles Champion:
Gardnar Mulloy, 43 years, 226 days (1957)
Oldest Mixed Doubles Champion:
Sherwood Stewart, 42 years, 28 days (1988)
Youngest Men's Singles Seed:
Bjorn Borg, 17 years, 19 days (no. 6 in 1973)
Oldest Men's Singles Seed:
Pancho Gonzalez, 41 years, 211 days (no. 12 in 1969)

Pete Sampras held the world no 1 ranking for the longest
period, 286 weeks. Boris Becker held it for only 12 weeks.

The longest set was played in 1969 between Pancho Gonzales
and Charlie Pasarell. Gonzalez won 22-24, 1-6, 16-14, 6-3, 11-
9 in 5 hours and 12 minutes. This was in the pre tie-break era.

MULTIPLE MEN'S SINGLES WINNERS AT WIMBLEDON

William Renshaw, **7**, 1881, 1882, 1883, 1884, 1885, 1886, 1887
Pete Sampras, **7**, 1993, 1994, 1995, 1997, 1998, 1999, 2000

Laurie Doherty, **5**, 1902, 1903, 1904, 1905, 1906
Bjorn Borg, **5**, 1976, 1977, 1978, 1979, 1980

Reggie Doherty, **4**, 1897, 1898, 1899, 1900
Anthony Wilding, **4**, 1910, 1911, 1912, 1913
Rod Laver, **4**, 1961, 1962, 1968, 1969

Wilfred Baddeley, **3**, 1891, 1892, 1895
Arthur Gore, **3**, 1901, 1908, 1909
Bill Tilden, **3**, 1920, 1921, 1930
Frederick Perry, **3**, 1934, 1935, 1936
John Newcombe, **3**, t 1967, 1970, 1971
John McEnroe, **3**, 1981, 1983, 1984
Boris Becker, **3**, 1985, 1986, 1989

John Hartley, **2**, 1879, 1880
Joshua Pim, **2**, 1893, 1894
Norman Brookes, **2**, 1907, 1914
Gerald Patterson, **2**, 1919, 1922
Jean Borotra, **2**, 1924, 1926
Rene Lacoste, **2**, 1925, 1928
Henri Cochet, **2**, 1927, 1929
Don Budge, **2**, 1937, 1938
Lew Hoad, **2**, 1956, 1957
Roy Emerson, **2**, 1964, 1965
Jimmy Connors, **2**, 1974, 1982
Stefan Edberg, **2**, 1988, 1990
Roger Federer, **2**, 2003, 2004

LADIES' SINGLES CHAMPIONS

1884–1885	Maud Watson
1886	Blanche Bingley
1887–1888	Charlotte Dod
1889	Blanche Bingley Hillyard
1890	Lena Rice
1891–1893	Charlotte Dod
1894	Blanche Bingley Hillyard
1895–1896	Charlotte Cooper
1897	Blanche Bingley Hillyard
1898	Charlotte Cooper
1899–1900	Blanche Bingley Hillyard
1901	Charlotte Cooper Sterry
1902	Muriel Robb
1903–1904	Dorothea Douglass
1905	May Sutton
1906	Dorothea Douglass
1907	May Sutton
1908	Charlotte Cooper Sterry
1909	Dora Boothby
1910–1911	Dorothea Lambert Chambers
1912	Ethel Thomson Larcombe
1913–1914	Dorothea Lambert Chambers
1915–1918	*not played*
1919–1923	Suzanne Lenglen
1924	Kathleen McKane
1925	Suzanne Lenglen
1926	Kathleen Godfree
1927–1930	Helen Wills Moody
1931	Cilly Aussem
1932–1933	Helen Wills Moody
1934	D. E. Round

1935	Helen Wills Moody
1936	Helen Jacobs
1937	D. E. Round
1938	Helen Wills Moody
1939	Alice Marble
1946	Pauline M. Betz
1947	Margaret Osborne
1948-1950	A. Louise Brough
1951	Doris Hart
1952-1954	Maureen Connolly
1955	A. Louise Brough
1956	Shirley Fry
1957-1958	Althea Gibson
1959-1960	Maria Bueno
1961	Angela Mortimer
1962	Karen Susman
1963	Margaret Smith
1964	Maria Bueno
1965	Margaret Smith
1966-1968	Billie Jean King
1969	Ann Jones
1970	Margaret Court
1971	Evonne Goolagong
1972-1973	Billie Jean King
1974	Chris Evert
1975	Billie Jean King
1976	Chris Evert
1977	Virginia Wade
1978-1979	Martina Navratilova
1980	Evonne Goolagong Cawley
1981	Chris Evert-Lloyd
1982-1987	Martina Navratilova

1988–1989	Steffi Graf
1990	Martina Navratilova
1991–1993	Steffi Graf
1994	Conchita Martinez
1995–1996	Steffi Graf
1997	Martina Hingis
1998	Jana Novotna
1999	Lindsay Davenport
2000–2001	Venus Williams
2002–2003	Serena Williams
2004	Maria Sharapova
2005	....
2006	....
2007	....
2008	....

"If she gets the jitters now, then she isn't the great champion that she is"
Max Robertson

"...and when Chrissie is playing well I always feel that she is playing well"
Anne Jones.

The women's champion receives a silver gilt salver made in 1864 by Messrs. Elkington and Co. Ltd of Birmingham. It is a copy of a pewter original in the Louvre, Paris. Since 1949 all champions have received a miniature replica of the trophy (diameter 8"/19cm).

Ladies' singles have been won by representatives of the following countries:

United States (49),
British Isles/Great Britain (36),
Germany (8),
France (6),
Australia (5),
Brazil (3),
Czechoslovakia/Czech Republic (3),
Spain (1),
Switzerland (1).

There have been five British ladies' champions since Wimbledon moved to Church Road – Kitty McKane Godfree, Dorothy Round, Angela Mortimer, Ann Jones and Virginia Wade.

LADIES' DOUBLES WINNERS

1913	Winifred McNair/Dora Boothby
1914	Agatha Morton/Elizabeth Ryan
1915-1918	*not played*
1919-1923	Suzanne Lenglen/Elizabeth Ryan
1924	Hazel Wightman/Helen Wills
1925	Suzanne Lenglen/Elizabeth Ryan
1926	Mary Browne/Elizabeth Ryan
1927	Helen Wills/Elizabeth Ryan
1928-1929	Peggy Saunders/Phoebe Watson
1930	Helen Wills Moody/Elizabeth Ryan
1931	Phyllis Mudford/Dorothy S. Barron
1932	Doris Metaxa/Josane Sigart
1933-1934	Simone Mathieu/Elizabeth Ryan
1935-1936	Freda James/Kay Stammers
1937	Simone Mathieu/Billie Yorke
1938-1939	Sarah Fabyan/Alice Marble
1940-1945	*not played*
1946	Louise Brough/Margaret duPont
1947	Patricia Todd/Doris Hart
1948-1950	Louise Brough/Margaret duPont
1951-1953	Doris Hart/Shirley Fry
1954	Louise Brough/Margaret duPont
1955	Angela Mortimer/Anne Shilcock
1956	Angela Buxton/Althea Gibson
1957	Althea Gibson/Darlene Hard
1958	Maria Bueno/Althea Gibson
1959	Jeanne Arth/Darlene Hard
1960	Maria Bueno/Darlene Hard
1961-1962	Karen Hantze Susman/Bille Jean Moffitt
1963	Maria Bueno/Darlene Hard
1964	Margaret Smith/Lesley Turner
1965	Maria Bueno/Billie Jean King

1966	Maria Bueno/Nancy Richey
1967-1968	Rosie Casals/Billie Jean King
1969	Margaret Smith Court/Judy Tegart Dalton
1970-1971	Rosie Casals/Billie Jean King
1972	Billie Jean King/Betty Stove
1973	Rosie Casals/Billie Jean King
1974	Evonne Goolagong/Peggy Michel
1975	Ann Kiyomura/Kazuko Sawamatsu
1976	Chris Evert/Martina Navratilova
1977	Helen Gourlay Cawley/JoAnne Russell
1978	Kerry Reid/Wendy Turnbull
1979	Billie Jean King/Martina Navratilova
1980	Kathy Jordan/Anne Smith
1981-1984	Martina Navratilova/Pam Shriver
1985	Kathy Jordan/Elizabeth Smylie
1986	Martina Navratilova/Pam Shriver
1987	Claudia Kohde-Kilsch/Helena Sukova
1988	Steffi Graf/Gabriela Sabatini
1989-1990	Jana Novotna/Helena Sukova
1991	Larisa Neiland/Natasha Zvereva
1992-1994	Gigi Fernandez/Natasha Zvereva
1995	Jana Novotna/Arantxa Sanchez Vicario
1996	Martina Hingis/Helena Sukova
1997	Gigi Fernandez/Natasha Zvereva
1998	Martina Hingis/Jana Novotna
1999	Lindsay Davenport/Corina Morariu
2000	Venus Williams/Serena Williams
2001	Lisa Raymond/Rennae Stubbs
2002	Serena Williams/Venus Williams
2003	Kim Clijsters/Ai Sugiyama
2004	Cara Black/Rennae Stubbs
2005	....
2006	....
2007	....

Some facts About the Ladies

Maud Watson was the first ladies' champion and 13 other women took part in the first ladies' competition, all of them British. Miss Watson set the fashion for wearing white, in an ankle-length white woolen skirt (and a sailor-hat).

Lottie Dod lost a competition final to Maud Watson when she was still only 13. The following year (1887), at age 15, she won Wimbledon. Lottie was also a member of the British national field hockey team in 1899, the British Amateur golf champion in 1904, a silver medalist in archery at the 1908 Olympics, did the Cresta run, and was good at skating, rowing, horse-riding, billiards, playing the piano and singing. She retired from tennis at age 21 having lost only one competitive match since age 15.

Blanch Bingley won Wimbledon 6 times between 1886 and 1900, her 6th at age 36; she made her last Wimbledon appearance at age 49.

May Sutton of the United States became the first non-European Wimbledon champion in 1905 when she won the women's singles title, causing a stir by rolling up her sleeves on court! She won again in 1907. She was born in Plymouth, UK. She later coached her daughter Dorothy Bundy who became the first American to win the Australian Open in 1938.

In the 1919 ladies' final Lambert Chambers wore a dark grey dress with starched white collar and cuffs. In 1920 Suzanne

Lenglen (France) broke with tradition by not wearing a corset and in 1927 Ruth Tapscott of South Africa became the first woman to play without wearing stockings.

The winner of the most ladies' doubles championships was Miss E.M. Ryan (USA) winning 12 titles in 1914, 1919-1923, 1925-1927, 1930, 1933, 1934

Suzanne Lenglen (France) was the star of the 1920s, winning 12 Grand Slam titles, 6 at Wimbledon, and 17 doubles. She quit amateur tennis in 1926 after "a mix-up" caused her to keep the King and Queen of England waiting; it is said that they were not amused…

In 1926 Kitty McCane (married name Godfree) and her husband Leslie became the first and only husband and wife pair to win mixed doubles at Wimbledon.

Helen Wills Moody won seven American championships, eight Wimbledon titles, and four French titles. There was a record interval of 15 years between her first and last Grand Slam title wins. On the court she was inscrutable. She rarely spoke to an opponent but stared out from an expressionless face that was generally topped by a green-lined white eyeshade. Her nickname was "Little Miss Poker Face".

Britain's Dorothy Round was the first non-Australian woman to win the Open there, in 1935. She won mixed doubles at Wimbledon with Fred Perry in 1935 and 1936 but because of her religious beliefs, refused to play on a Sunday.

Alice Marble was remarkable in that she won 5 Grand Slam titles between 1936 and 1940 after having suffered a severe bout of tuberculosis. She was the first woman to wear shorts at Wimbledon, taking the title in 1939.

American Pauline Betz was refused permission to defend her Wimbledon title in 1947 because she was having discussions about turning professional.

When Gussie Moran wore a short, lace-trimmed skirt in 1949 she was accused by the AELTC of 'bringing vulgarity and sin into tennis'. Her outfit had been designed by Ted Tinling who was, at the time, an umpire. The resulting furore cost him his Wimbledon job but opened the door to his new career as a dress designer.

In 1953 Maureen "Little Mo" Connolly became the first woman to achieve a calendar-year Grand Slam at age 18 and was the youngest-ever winner of the US Open at age 16. In 3 visits to Wimbledon she never lost a match. She took up tennis because her family could not afford to continue paying for her horse-riding lessons. Her career was ended at age 19 in a horse-riding accident which badly damaged one of her legs.

Althea Gibson (USA) became the first black player to win a Wimbledon singles championship when she captured the title in 1957. Until age 23 she was not allowed to compete in the US championships.

Maria Bueno of Brazil achieved a calendar-year doubles Grand Slam in 1960.

Angela Mortimer took the women's title in 1961 at her 11th attempt. She beat Christine Truman in the first all-British final since 1914.

Anne Jones (UK) was the first left-hander to win the ladies' singles at Wimbledon, in 1969, using an aluminium racket.

In 1970 Margaret Court (Australia) became the second woman to win a calendar year Grand Slam and the first Australian woman to win Wimbledon. She won a record total of 62 Grand Slam titles and won the Grand Slam in mixed doubles with Ken Fletcher. She is now a priest.

Chris Evert introduced the two-handed backhand to the ladies' game. She spent 262 weeks as world no 1.

Virginia Wade (Britain) played in 25 Wimbledons, taking the singles title in 1977, the 100th anniversary of the championships.

"Chris Lloyd came out of the dressing room like a pistol"
Virginia Wade

"It's quite clear that Virginia Wade is thriving on the pressure now that the pressure on her to do well is off"
Harry Carpenter

The last married woman to win the women's singles was Chris Evert Lloyd in 1981. The last mother to win was Evonne Goolagong, in 1980; she also won in 1971 and was beaten in 3 finals in between.

Chris Evert won her first Grand Slam as a 20 year old in 1974 but was almost as famous for being Jimmy Connors' girlfriend. From 1974 – 1986 she won at least one Grand Slam title per year, a record 13 consecutive years. (Steffi Graf is second with 12 consecutive winning years.) In all she won 18 Grand Slam championships. She holds the record for the most Grand Slam appearances, 34 – and the most finals lost, 18.

Tracy Austin (USA) and her brother were the first brother-sister champions winning the Wimbledon mixed doubles, in 1980. She was the youngest US Open winner at 16 years 271 days.

Billie Jean King won a record 20 Wimbledon titles including all 3 in 1967 and 1973. She won 39 Grand Slam titles in all. Billie Jean was the oldest woman to receive a singles seed at Wimbledon at the age of 39 in 1983. She was seeded no 10. She was the first tennis player to openly admit to being gay.

Tennis is a perfect combination of violent action taking place in an atmosphere of total tranquility.'   Billie Jean King

Jennifer Capriati turned professional before her 14th birthday in 1990 and at that age became the youngest-ever Grand Slam semi-finalist. She won Olympic gold at 16. Drugs and shoplifting offences interrupted her career in the late 1990s but she made a comeback to win the French and Australian Opens in 2001.

Steffi Graf's full name is Stefanie Maria Graf. She is one of only 3 women to achieve the Grand Slam and won 22 individual championships in all (only Margaret Court beats her, with 24). She is the only player (man or woman) to win all 4 Grand Slam titles twice in two decades and she also won Olympic gold in 1988. Steffi Graf won at least seven tournaments a year for eleven straight years 1986-96. She married Andre Agassi in 2001

Monica Seles (Yugoslavia) became the youngest Grand Slam title winner, at Roland Garros in 1990, aged 16 years and 169 days. She was stabbed on court in Hamburg in 1993 by a mentally-ill fan of Steffi Graf. She has reached only one major final since recovering from that attack.

Mary Pierce won 2 Grand Slam titles in 1995 and 2000. She was born in Canada, raised in USA and won her titles as a French national.

Lindsay Davenport won Olympic Gold in 1996, three years before winning her first Wimbledon title, the tallest woman to do so.

Martina Hingis, ladies singles winner in 1997, was named after Martina Navratilova. Both come from former Czechoslovakia. She was the youngest-ever Grand Slam junior champion winning at Roland Garros in 1993 at age 12. She won the Australian singles and doubles in 3 consecutive years.

Martina Navratilova is the oldest person, male or female, to win a Grand Slam title, taking the Australian Open and the Wimbledon mixed doubles in 2003, at age 46. She holds 18 Grand Slam titles, only beaten by Margaret Court, Helen Wills Moody and Steffi Graf. A record 32 years separates her first and latest Grand Slam appearances and she met Chris Evert in a record 14 finals over 11 years. She won the ladies' singles at Wimbledon 9 times. Martina defected from then communist Czechoslovakia to USA in 1975 leaving the no 1 position back home to Hana Mandlikova.

Venus Williams has an endorsement deal with Reebok believed to be worth a record-breaking $40 million (£22 million). In 2000 she won 35 matches in succession and took Wimbledon, the US Open and Olympic gold. She also won doubles gold with her sister Serena.

"Billie Jean King, with the look on her face that says she can't believe it... because she never believes it, and yet, somehow, I think she does"
Max Robertson

"She comes from a tennis-playing family. Her father's a dentist."
BBC 2

LADIES' WIMBLEDON RECORDS

Most Women's Singles Titles:
Martina Navratilova, **9**, (1978,1979,1982, 1985, 1987, 1990)
Most Women's Doubles Titles:
Elizabeth Ryan, **12**, (1914, 1919-23, 1925-27,
1930, 1933-34)
Most Mixed Doubles Titles (Women):
Elizabeth Ryan, **7**, (1919, 1921, 1923, 1927-28,
1930, 1932)
Most Singles, Doubles, and Mixed Doubles Titles (Women):
Billie Jean King, **20**, (6 singles, 10 doubles, 4 mixed, 1961-79)
Youngest Women's Singles Champion:
Charlotte Dod, 15 years, 285 days (1887)
Youngest Women's Doubles Champion:
Martina Hingis, 15 years, 282 days (1996)
Youngest Mixed Doubles Champion:
Tracy Austin, 17 years, 206 days (1980)
Oldest Women's Singles Champion:
Charlotte Sterry, 37 years, 282 days (1908)
Oldest Women's Doubles Champion:
Elizabeth Ryan, 42 years, 152 days (1934)
Oldest Mixed Doubles Champion:
Martina Navratilova, 46 years, 259 days (2003)
Youngest Women's Singles Seed:
Jennifer Capriati, 14 years, 89 days (no. 12 in 1990)
Most Matches Played at The Championships:
313 Martina Navratilova (TCH/USA) 1973-2004 (Singles
W 120, L 14; Doubles W 93, L 19; Mixed W 54 L 13)

The longest period ranked as world no 1 goes to Steffi Graf
who held the position for 377 weeks, followed by Martina
Navratilova with 331 weeks. Jennifer Capriati was there for 3
weeks.

SOME STATISTICS ABOUT THE LADIES AT WIMBLEDON

Winners of Singles, Doubles, Mixed Doubles
Wimbledon Championships in One Year
1920 Miss S.R.F. Lenglen (FRA)
1922 Miss S.R.F. Lenglen (FRA)
1925 Miss S.R.F. Lenglen (FRA)
1939 Miss A. Marble (USA)
1948 Miss A.L. Brough (USA)
1950 Miss A.L. Brough (USA)
1951 Miss D.J. Hart (USA)
1967 Mrs. L.W. King (USA)
1973 Mrs. L.W. King (USA)

The Youngest Competitors
Singles M. Klima (Austria) 13 years (1997)
Doubles JenniferCapriati (USA) 14 years, 92 days (1990)

The Oldest Competitors
Singles Mrs. A.E. O'Neill (GBR) 54 years, 304 days (1922)
Doubles Mrs. C.O. Tuckey (GBR) 54 years, 352 days (1932)
Mixed Doubles Mrs. A.E. O'Neil (GBR) 55 years,
304 days (1923)

The Youngest Seed
Singles Jennifer Capriati (USA) 14 years, 89 days (1990)

The Oldest Seed
Singles Billie Jean King (USA) 39 years, 210 days (1983)

Shortest Player
Miss C.G. Hoahing (GBR)
1937-1938 4 feet, 9½ inches (1.46m)

Tallest Player
Lindsay Davenport (USA) 1993,2001 6 feet 2½ inches(1.89m)

MULTIPLE TITLE WINNERS

Martina Navratilova, **9**, 1978, 1979, 1982, 1983, 1984, 1985, 1986, 1987,1990

Helen Wills Moody, **8**, 1927, 1928, 1929, 1930, 1932, 1933, 1935, 1938

Steffi Graf, **7**, 1988, 1989, 1991, 1992, 1993, 1995, 1996
Dorothea Lambert Chambers, **7**, 1903, 1904, 1906, 1910, 1911, 1913, 1914

Blanche Bingley Hillyard, **6**, 1886, 1889, 1894, 1897, 1899, 1900
Suzanne Lenglen, **6**, 1919, 1920, 1921, 1922, 1923, 1925
Billie Jean King, **6**, 1966, 1967, 1968, 1972, 1973, 1975

Charlotte Dod, **5**, 1887, 1888, 1891, 1892, 1893
Charlotte Cooper Sterry, **5**, 1895, 1896, 1898, 1901, 1908

Louise Brough, **4**, 1948, 1949, 1950, 1955

Dorothea Lambert Chambers, **3**, 1910, 1911, 1913, 1914
Maria Bueno, **3**, 1959, 1960, 1964
Maureen Connolly, **3**, 1952, 1953, 1954
Dorothea Douglass, **3**, 1903, 1904, 1906
Margaret Smith Court, **3**, 1963, 1965, 1970
Chris Evert Lloyd, **3**, 1974, 1976, 1981

Maud Watson, **2**, 1884, 1885
May Sutton, **2**, 1905, 1907
Kathleen McKane Godfree, **2**, 1924, 1926
Dorothy Round, **2**, 1934, 1937
Althea Gibson, **2**, 1957, 1958
Evonne Goolagong Cawley, **2**, 1971, 1980
Venus Williams, **2**, 2000, 2001
Serena Williams, **2**, 2002, 2003

MIXED DOUBLES WINNERS

1914	James Parke/Ethel Thomson Larcombe
1915–1918	*not played*
1919	Randolph Lycett/Elizabeth Ryan
1920	Gerald Patterson/Suzanne Lenglen
1921	Randolph Lycett/Elizabeth Ryan
1922	Pat O'Hara Wood/Suzanne Lenglen
1923	Randolph Lycett/Elizabeth Ryan
1924	John Gilbert/Kathleen McKane
1925	Jean Borotra/Suzanne Lenglen
1926	Leslie Godfree/Kathleen McKane Godfree
1927	Frank Hunter/Elizabeth Ryan
1928	Patrick Spence/Elizabeth Ryan
1929	Frank Hunter/Helen Wills
1930	Jack Crawford/Elizabeth Ryan
1931	George Lott/Anna Harper
1932	Enrique Maier/Elizabeth Ryan
1933	Gottfried von Cramm/Hilde Krahwinkel
1934	Ryuki Miki/Dorothy Round
1935–1936	Fred Perry/Dorothy Round
1937–1938	Don Budge/Alice Marble
1939	Bobby Riggs/Alice Marble
1940–1945	*not played*
1946	Tom Brown/Louise Brough
1947–1948	John Bromwich/Louise Brough
1949	Eric Sturgess/Sheila Summers
1950	Eric Sturgess/Louise Brough
1951–1952	Frank Sedgman/Doris Hart
1953–1956	Vic Seixas/Doris Hart
1957	Mervyn Rose/Darlene Hard
1958	Robert Howe/Lorraine Coghlan
1959–1960	Rod Laver/Darlene Hard

1961	Fred Stolle/Lesley Turner
1962	Neale Fraser/Margaret duPont
1963	Ken Fletcher/Margaret Smith
1964	Fred Stolle/Lesley Turner
1965-1966	Ken Fletcher/Margaret Smith
1967	Owen Davidson/Billie Jean Moffitt King
1968	Ken Fletcher/Margaret Court
1969	Fred Stolle/Ann Haydon Jones
1970	Ilie Nastase/Rosie Casals
1971	Owen Davidson/Billie Jean King
1972	Ilie Nastase/Rosie Casals
1973-1974	Owen Davidson/Billie Jean King
1975	Marty Riessen/Margaret Court
1976	Tony Roche/Francoise Durr
1977	Bob Hewitt/Greer Stevens
1978	Frew McMillan/Betty Stove
1979	Bob Hewitt/Greer Stevens
1980	John Austin/Tracy Austin
1981	Frew McMillan/Betty Stove
1982	Kevin Curren/Anne Smith
1983-1984	John Lloyd/Wendy Turnbull
1985	Paul McNamee/Martina Navratilova
1986	Ken Flach/Kathy Jordan
1987	Michael Bates/Jo Durie
1988	Sherwood Stewart/Zina Garrison
1989	Jim Pugh/Jana Novotna
1990	Rick Leach/Zina Garrison
1991	John Fitzgerald/Elizabeth Smylie
1992	Cyril Suk/Larisa Neiland
1993	Mark Woodforde/Martina Navratilova
1994	Todd Woodbridge/Helena Sukova
1995	Jonathan Stark/Martina Navratilova
1996-1997	Cyril Suk/Helena Sukova

1998	Max Mirnyi/Serena Williams
1999	Leander Paes/Lisa Raymond
2000	Donald Johnson/Kimberly Po
2001	L Friedl/Daniela Hantuchova
2002	Mahesh Bhupathi/Elena Likhovtseva
2003	Leander Paes/Martina Navratilova
2004	Todd Woodbridge/Alicia Molik
2005	....
2006	....
2007	....
2008	....

GRAND SLAM WINNERS

The Grand Slam winners:
Australian Open, French Open, Wimbledon and U.S. Open
in the same calendar year:

1938 – Don Budge, United States
1953 – Maureen Connolly, United States
1962 – Rod Laver, Australia
1969 – Rod Laver, Australia
1970 – Margaret Smith Court, Australia
1988 – Steffi Graf, West Germany

● In 1938, Budge defeated John Bromwich in the Australian final, Roderick Menzel in the French, Henry Austin at Wimbledon and Gene Mako in the U.S. Open to complete his Grand Slam.

● In 1953, Maureen Connolly defeated Julia Sampson in the Australian final and Doris Hart in the French, Wimbledon and U.S. Open finals to complete her Grand Slam at age 18.

• In 1962, Laver defeated Roy Emerson in the Australian and French finals, Marty Mulligan at Wimbledon and Emerson again in the U.S. Open to complete his Grand Slam.

• In 1969, Laver defeated Andres Gimeno in the Australian final, Ken Rosewall in the French, John Newcombe at Wimbledon and Tony Roche in the U.S. Open to complete his Grand Slam.

• In 1970, Smith defeated Kerry Melville in the Australian final, Helga Niessen in the French, Billie Jean King at Wimbledon and Rosie Casals at the U.S. Open to complete her Grand Slam.

• In 1988, Steffi Graf defeated Chris Evert in the Australian final, Natalia Zvereva in the French, Martina Navratilova at Wimbledon and Gabriela Sabatini at the U.S. Open to complete her Grand Slam. Graf also defeated Gabriela Sabatini to win the gold medal at the 1988 Olympics in Seoul and complete the "golden" slam.

PLAYERS WHO HAVE WON ALL FOUR GRAND SLAM TITLES

MEN	WOMEN
Andre Agassi	Maureen Connolly
Don Budge	Chris Evert Lloyd
Roy Emerson	Shirley Fry
Rod Laver	Steffi Graf
Fred Perry	Doris Hart
	Billie Jean King
	Martina Navratilova
	Margaret Smith Court
	Serena Williams

THE CHAMPIONSHIP TODAY

The Championships are run by the 12-member AELTC Committee plus 7 nominees from the Lawn Tennis Association (LTA). Preparation for The Championships begins directly after the preceding meeting.

The order of play is selected by a process of "draws" or "round robins"

The Championships Events comprise:
Gentlemen's Singles
Ladies' Singles
Gentlemen's Doubles
Ladies' Doubles
Mixed Doubles
Boys' Doubles
Girls' Singles
Girls' Doubles
35 and over Gentlemen's Invitation Doubles
45 and over Gentlemen's Invitation Doubles
35 and over Ladies' Invitation Doubles

Approximately 650 matches are played during the Fortnight

Around 15,000 balls are used during the tournament and new balls are provided after 5-7 games. Slazenger has provided every tennis ball for the championships at Wimbledon since 1902.

——————— QUALIFYING TO PLAY ———————

Players submit their entry at least six weeks before the competition begins. The committee together with the referee use computer rankings to select the players to be admitted directly, those who have to qualify and those who are rejected. About 500 entries, including juniors, are accepted with 128 included in the draw for the men's and ladies' singles, 64 pairs for the men's and the ladies' doubles and 48 pairs for the mixed doubles.

Qualifying competitions to select those players who have to qualify have been staged since 1925. Until 1966 there were separate qualifying competitions in the North and South of England. This was done to keep down the costs for the players, who were all unpaid amateurs. Since 1966 all qualifiers have been held at The Bank of England Sports Ground, Priory Lane, Roehampton, in South-West London.

Players wishing to enter the singles' events at Wimbledon have to play three rounds on grass at Roehampton and the prize for success is entry into the main Wimbledon draw, the following week. There is no single 'winner' of the qualifying matches. Instead the players who win all three rounds, sixteen in the gentlemen's singles and twelve in the ladies', will progress together with four pairs in each of the ladies' and men's doubles. All players entering the qualifying competition receive prize money.

In 1977 the eighteen year-old John MacEnroe was a qualifier and reached the semi-finals of the men's singles, which he lost to Jimmy Connors. Alexandra Stevenson (USA) was a qualifier in 1999. She beat the Yugoslav, Jelena Dokic, who, unusually, was also a qualifier, in the quarter-finals. Stevenson lost in the semi-finals to Lindsay Davenport, who won the title that year.

Lucky losers are losers in the last round of qualifying competitions, chosen in order of world rankings to fill any vacancy which occurs in the draw before the first round has been completed, typically when a selected player withdraws.

Wild cards are players whose world-ranking does not guarantee them a place and who are accepted directly into the competition at the discretion of the committee either because of past performance at Wimbledon or (economics speaking here?) to increase British interest in the fortnight. Wild Cards have been allocated since 1977.

Goran Ivanisevic in 2001 is the only wild card to have won the men's singles title and no wild card has won the ladies' singles.

The Junior Events are held during the second week of Wimbledon. National tennis associations affiliated to the International Tennis Federation submit the entries and a qualifying competition is held.

35 and 45 & Over events take place during the second week of Wimbledon. The invitation goes to all players of the relevant age who in the previous 20 years have reached th semi-final or final of the singles and/or the final of the doubles. The final selection, including 'wild cards', is at the discretion of the Committee.

SEEDING

Seeding was introduced in 1924 and in 1927 competitors were selected for the first time according to ability irrespective of nationality. Seeding has been based on computer rankings since 1975. The top 32 men and women players are seeded.

Unseeded players won the men's singles in 1985 and 2001. No unseeded player has ever won the ladies' singles. Eleven unseeded players have reached the final of the men's singles and four unseeded players the ladies'. Nine unseeded pairs have won the men's doubles, five unseeded pairs have won the ladies' doubles and ten unseeded pairs have won the mixed doubles.

Courts are repaired and re-seeded each Summer and early Autumn.

"These ball boys are marvellous. You don't even notice them. There's a left handed one over there. I noticed him earlier."
Max Robertson

OFFICIALS, UMPIRES, BALL-BOYS

There are approximately 270 British and 60 overseas officials from 27 countries.

There are around 330 officials at the championships working as chair umpires, line umpires or off-court staff. Around 45 chair umpires are assigned for each day, with the other officials working as line umpires. Chair umpires normally umpire two matches a day, although not necessarily on the same court. Line umpires work in teams and there are two line teams per court. who work 75 minutes on, 75 minutes off. 10 Line umpires work on each of Centre, No.1 and No. 2 courts and 7 on each of the other courts.

The Referee's decision on a question of law is final and he can overrule the umpire.

Cyclops was introduced in 1980. This is a device which transmits infra-red rays across the court to make close service line calls on Centre, No.1 and No.2 courts. Cyclops was invented by Bill Carlton of Malta.

Net cord judges are no longer used at Wimbledon. Instead there is a sensitive electronic net cord machine operated by the chair umpire and it is this machine which makes the familiar beep if the ball touches the net.

HAWK-EYE

The BBC introduced the Hawk-Eye technology
for the first time at Wimbledon in 2003. Hawk-Eye
uses the latest camera and computer technology
to track the ball on the court. Taking into account
the trajectory, skid and compression of the ball,
Hawk-Eye produces an accurate real-time computer
generated replay which can be viewed and replayed
through 360 degrees.

These graphic representations
of the ball's path can be used by
the commentators to illustrate
a whole host of statistics and
player characteristics, from the
trajectory of a player's serve to
the distribution of a player's
return.

Owned by The Television Corporation Plc.,
Hawk-Eye was developed initially for cricket.
In tennis Hawk-Eye is mainly used to analyse
patterns of play, highlighting player performance
and match strategy - therefore helping to explain
the game and increase viewers' understanding
of the intricacies of the sport.

It is used specifically to analyse:

1. Serve Direction
Hawk-Eye graphics illustrate the bounce point of serves,
colour-coded by Ace, first serve and second serve

2. Break Point Analysis
illustrates the bounce point of all serves in play while
the serve is at break point.

3. Ace Analysis
illustrates the trajectory and bounce point of all Aces.

4. Service Trajectory
illustrates the trajectory of a player's serve.

5. Return Hit Point
shows the hit point of all returns of serve, with each
return colour coded by first serve return or second serve
return.

6. Rally Hit Point
shows the hit point for all strokes (excluding serve and
return) which were hit into play.

7. Rally Direction
shows the bounce point of all strokes in play (excluding
serve and return).

8. Baseline Winners
shows the speed and trajectory of each baseline winner.

A secondary use for Hawk-Eye can be to offer an
alternative view on a contentious line call decision,
illustrating whether or not a ball went out of play.
This is not available to umpires and will only be used
if a decision has been contested by either player or
occasionally where there has been an over-rule.

Chair Umpires first replaced the scorecard with a computer in 2001.

Approximately 200 ball boys and ball girls are chosen from around 300 applicants. Ball girls were first introduced in 1977 and the boy/girl ratio is now 50/50. The first mixed teams of ball boys and girls were used in 1988. Ball girls appeared on Centre Court for the first time in 1985.

It is a common misconception that ball boys and girls are selected from residents at Dr. Barnardo's homes. This was the case from the 1930's until the 1960's (when they were also selected from residents of Shaftesbury Homes) but since then they have come from local schools.

TICKETS

A ballot for tickets was first introduced in 1922 and since then demand has always exceeded supply.

Many advance tickets are sold through The Lawn Tennis Association and to foreign tennis associations

Each day approximately 500 Centre Court (except for the last 4 days), no.1 and no.2 court tickets are reserved for sale at the turnstiles. Approximately 6,000 ground tickets are available each day for that day's play. Some visitors queue all night to get these tickets.

You can queue all night but tickets are available strictly on the basis of one per person queuing and payment is by cash only.

Ground tickets cost around £16 (US$ 28) each but fall in price during the second week. Centre, no 1 and no 2 tickets cost from £25 - £30 (US$ 44 - $53) in the first week, rising to £50 (US$ 88) or more in the second.

───────── ODDS & ENDS ─────────

Radio commentaries were first broadcast in 1927.

Wimbledon introduced its own radio station, Radio Wimbledon, in 1992, broadcasting throughout the Championships on 87.7 FM.

Each year around 24 tons of strawberries, 8 tons of salmon and 15,000 bottles of champagne are consumed at Wimbledon.

─────────

"McEnroe has got to sit down and work out where he stands"
Fred Perry

"And here's Zivojinovic, six foot six inches tall and fourteen pounds ten ounces"
Dan Maskell

Wimbledon Windmill, 1893

WIMBLEDON

─── THE PLACE ───

"much the finest place about" Jonathan Swift (1713)

The current spelling of the "village" name is well-known. Earlier versions include:
Wipandune, Wibbandune, Wunemannedun, Wimeldon, Wimmeldun, Wimbaldus, Wymbaldon, Wymbaldone, Wymbeldon, Wimbleton. The suffix —dun, -tun, -ton, -don etc., is the ancient root of our modern word "town". There is also a Latin root "dunum", a "hill position" from which our modern word "dune" is derived, and Wimbledon, sited on a hill, could also have this word as part of its roots.

In the middle ages Wimbledon belonged to the Archbishops of Canterbury and was part of the manor of Mortlake, which included modern-day Putney, Roehampton, East Sheen, Wimbledon and Mortlake. At this time Wimbledon was basically farmland.

In 1536 the manor was surrendered to the new Head of the Church of England, Henry VIII.

Wimbledon village has been part of the London Borough of Merton since 1965. Before that it was part of the county of Surrey.

BUILDINGS

(the letters signify the position on the map on the following pages)

The oldest "building" in Wimbledon is the remains of the earthworks known as Caesar's Camp (**A**) on the SW edge of the common. Although it has never been properly excavated it is believed to predate the Roman occupation of Britain. Caesar arrived in Britain in 55 BC. But the "camp" is thought now to date back to 600 – 800 BC. Since 1907 it has been within the grounds of The Royal Wimbledon Golf Club.

The oldest remaining inhabited building is The Old Rectory (**B**), which stands just north of St Mary's Church on the opposite side of Church Rd from the AELTC (**C**). It was built around 1500 on the site of a previous dwelling-house. In its early days this was a very grand house and has had some very grand owners, including Sir William Cecil, Secretary of State to Edward VI in the mid 1500's and subsequently adviser to Elizabeth I, and more recently rock guitarist Brian May.

A menu for a Sunday lunch with the Cecils included:
First Course: Brawn and mustard; Boiled meat stewed;
Boiled beef; pie; Veal or pig; roast capon.
Second course: Wild fowl or coney (rabbit); Lark or pigeon; tart
Not a vegetable in sight …

Around this time the Cecils planted in the Old Rectory gardens one of England's only two remaining fig-walks, a fifty yard (45 metres) long pair of rows of fig trees trained over a frame to create a tunnel.

Wimbledon Park, opposite the AELTC and substantially covered by car-parks during Wimbledon fortnight was originally part of the grounds of the great 17th Century manor house (**D**) built by the Cecil family (it burned down on Easter Monday, 1785). By the early 18th Century it was in the hands of Earl Spencer (as in Althorp, Princess Diana...) who employed Capability Brown to landscape it in 1765-68. He created the present lake (**E**) of 30 acres (12 hectares).

In 1846 the Spencer family sold the house and park but retained the title of Lord of the Manor.

The domed Well House (**F**) in Arthur Rd will be familiar to tennis visitors queuing on the Village side. It is the only remaining Wimbledon building erected by the Spencer family. It covered a well of originally only 30-40 feet (12 metres) dug to supply the manor house with water. It was deepened in 1798 to over 550 feet (170 metres) and when water was struck it shot 100 feet (30 metres) into the air. It silted up in the early 19th Century and the building is now a private house.

The church next to the rectory is the Parish Church of St Mary The Virgin (**G**) and it is probably the 4th church to stand on this site. It was built in 1788 though the nave and tower were reconstructed in the early 1840s and the chancel in

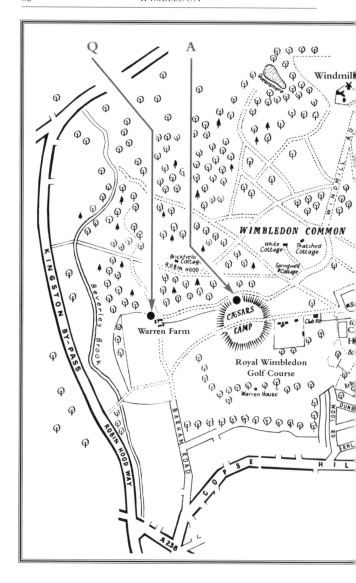

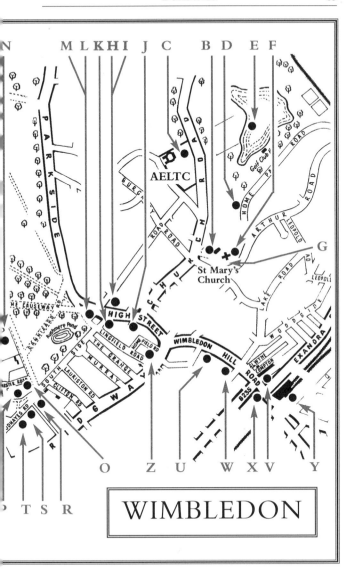

N M L K H I J C B D E F

AELTC

St Mary's
Church

G

PARKSIDE

HIGH STREET

WIMBLEDON HILL

O Z U W X V Y

P T S R

WIMBLEDON

*Parish Church of
St Mary The Virgin,
Wimbledon*

1860. Its spire is known around the world as it is shown at the beginning and the end of each Wimbledon tennis championship TV broadcast. The hammerbeam roof was added in the 1840s supported on iron girders carefully covered with plaster to make them look like stone pillars.

The Jacobean building now known as Eagle House (**H**) was built in the village in the early 1600's by Robert Bell, a wealthy merchant. The Eagle from which the house takes its modern name was not put onto the gable until 1860.

The Rose & Crown pub (**I**), next door to Eagle House was built around 1650. As England was going through a rare Republican phase at the time the original name was "The Rose"; the "Crown" was added some time in the 18th Century. The first regular stage-coach services to and from London started in 1790 from the Rose & Crown. The journey took about 2 hours each way, servicing Wimbledon's early commuters.

A survey of Wimbledon was published in 1617 which shows there was a bowling alley next to what is now the site of The Rose & Crown. There was a pub on the site of The Dog & Fox (**J**), opposite the end of Church Rd, so familiar to tennis-goers. It was known then as "The Sign of My Lord's Arms" and is the oldest inn in the village.

Pubs were originally known as "alehouses", private homes serving ale brewed on the premises, "taverns", serving ales, wine and food or "inns" which also provided accomodation. As most brewers used to be women it was quite normal for alehouses and taverns to be owned and run by women. In the 10th Century King Edgar decreed that there were too many such establishments and that they should be restricted to one per village. During the First World War various laws were introduced to curb alcohol consumption and it became illegal to buy someone else a drink.

When Wimbledon became part of London in 1965 it meant that pubs could stay open on Sundays until 11.00 pm whilst pubs in Surrey, the county to which it formerly belonged, still had to close at 10.30.

The Dog & Fox Inn

One of the earliest of the other surviving older houses in the village is Claremont House (**K**), built in around 1650, on the corner of Lingfield Rd and the High St.

One Daniel Mason developed the houses now known as The Green (**L**), at the SE corner of the Common, by the High Street in the 1840's. He made money from the rents and began to describe himself as a "land and estate agent", thus becoming Wimbledon's first Estate Agent.

The war memorial (**M**) at the SE corner of the Common was erected in 1921 on the edge of the old village green. During the Second World War, between 1940 and 1941, some 400 bombs fell on Wimbledon.

Some of the better-heeled visitors to the tennis stay at the Cannizaro Hotel (**N**). The less prosperous can still visit the publicly-owned gardens, known as Cannizaro Park. This was originally the garden of one of the grand houses standing on this site (next to the present-day Cannizaro Hotel) since before 1700 and known variously as The Warren, The Old Park and Westside House. The gardens of the next-door house, The Keir, were added in 1932 and in 1948 the park was sold to Wimbledon Corporation and remains a public park to this day.

Cannizaro is named for the Duke of Cannizaro (a tiny village in Sicily) a title which passed to the then owner of Warren House in 1832. The duke, *"a good-looking, intelligent, but penniless Sicilian of high birth"*, Francis Platamone, Count St Antonio, hardly spent any time there and the house was first referred to as Cannizaro House in a census some years after his death. The old Cannizaro House burnt down in 1900 and was totally rebuilt, but the name stuck.

The magnificent Chester House (**O**) on the corner of Southside and the Crooked Billett dates from the era of William & Mary (turn of the 17th and 18th Centuries). It may have been built by the Duke of York (later James II) for one of his mistresses. Tom Paine is known to have visited the house in the early 1800s. Barclays Bank saved Chester House from demolition, buying it as their headquarters at the outbreak of the Second World War. It now contains private housing.

The founder of Watneys breweries began his brewing career in The Crooked Billet, (**P**) the small street on the SW edge of the common which today houses a pub of the same name and another called The Hand in Hand.

Warren Farm (**Q**), down an unpaved private road SW of the main part of the Common is one of the oldest properties in the area. Mentioned in the survey of 1617 it was the place where the "warrener" or rabbit-farmer lived. He also looked after the fish-ponds fed by the Beverley Brook, which forms part of the boundary of the common along the playing fields adjoining the A3. Warren Farm is now a private house.

Kings College School (**R**), one of the best boys' schools in the UK, now in the large Victorian Gothic building and its neighbours on Southside, moved to this location from central London in 1897. The School Hall was built in 1899.

Just next to Kings, to the west, stands the intriguing Southside House, (**S**) formed from two elegant semi-detached houses over 100 years ago. The house is reputed to have played host to Nelson and Lady Hamilton (which seems unlikely) and its art collection, open occasionally for public viewing, includes some good paintings and reputedly the necklace worn by Marie Antoinette at the end of her life. The house belonged to the family of author Axel Munthe.

A little further along to the west stands Gothic Lodge (**T**), built in 1763. This was the first house in London to have electric lighting. Marconi tested his newly-invented "wireless telegraph" by sending messages from here to the central post office in London.

The road leading down the hill from Wimbledon Village to the station is now called Wimbledon Hill Road (since the mid 1800's). It was previously known as The Lane to Merton, Bishop's Hill then Wimbledon Lane. In 1943 certain local councillors proposed changing the name to *Stalin Avenue*, in recognition of "our brave Soviet ally".

The old horse trough at the top of the hill was put there in 1893 by the Metropolitan Drinking Fountain and Cattle Trough Association, founded in 1859 "for the amelioration of animal suffering and the promotion of habits of temperence among our itinerant and working population".

On the right as you come down the hill stands The White House (**U**), the only remaining example of the Victorian mansions which formerly graced this road. It was built in the 1860's and is said to be haunted by an elderly gentleman, immaculately dressed, with grey hair and piercing blue eyes, thought to be a member of the Jones family who lived in the house from the time it was built until the outbreak of the Second World War in 1939.

In 1887 the first "free library" (**V**) was opened at its current site at the corner of Wimbledon Hill Rd and Alexandra Rd. At its opening the library had a stock of 6,000 books and within a year one in twelve of the local population had registered to use its facilities.

Wimbledon High School (**W**), a private girls' school on the corner of Mansel Rd and Wimbledon Hill Rd, more or less opposite the library, also opened in the early 1800's funded by the Girls' Public Day Schools Trust which still owns it and a number of other girls' schools today.

At the bottom of the hill, on the right, before the station, is the local department store, Ely's (**X**). Joseph Ely opened his first store in 1876 on the corner of Alexandra Rd., more or less opposite the present shop, which he opened 10 years later. When the trams first linked Wimbledon with nearby towns in the early 20th Century, the tramline passing by Ely's store, tram conductors were known to have been "encouraged" by gifts of pullovers and gloves to shout "Ely's Corner!" at the appropriate point in the journey.

The present main railway station (**Y**) was built in 1930 and is the 5th to be built in less than 100 years, the original one dating from 1838. The District Line tube station was first added in 1889.

The first real local history of Wimbledon was published in 1865 by the clergyman Revd. William Bartlett. This book, and many others on local history, can still be obtained from the Wimbledon Society Museum (**Z**) at the corner of Lingfield Rd and Ridgway. The museum, founded in 1916, opens on Saturdays and Sundays from 2.30-5pm and entry is free. (for information on books about Wimbledon contact The Wimbledon Society Museum at wimbledonmuseum@yahoo.co.uk).

TRANSPORT

The advent of the railway link to London in the late 1830's began the transformation of Wimbledon in a similar way to many of London's other modern suburbs.

NIMBYism (*Not in my back yard*) was as rife then as now. The railway company first wanted to build their new line on a route further North than the one it now occupies. The Earl of Cottenham, however, decided that he did not want dirty, noisy trains near his house on Copse Hill and refused to sell his land. Thus the railway was built on the "low lands" to the South of the district.

The first 23 miles (40 kms) of railway, from Vauxhall to Woking, opened in 1838 and the first trip took 45 minutes. Once the line opened to the public trains ran every 2-3 hours, instead of the (approximately) every 5 minutes today.

Because of the influence of the railways Wimbledon's population rocketed in the late 19th Century:

1861   4,644

1871   9,087

1881   15,949

Mr Clark, a blacksmith's assistant working for the railway company in Wimbledon in the 1890's earned £1.00 (US$ 1.80) for a 6-day week working from 6 am– 5.30pm.

THE COMMON

The Common comprises some 1250 acres (525 hectares) of public land open to everyone for recreational use.

From the early middle ages the manorial court decided what the local tenants could do on the lands owned by the manor and not rented out for farming or other uses. In other words

Wimbledon Common, about 1850

the "Commons" were generally the poorest land in the manor. The locals acquired rights and protections under law because of their continuing use of these lands, which reduced the rights of the lords of the manor, preventing them, for instance, from selling commons for other use. This system prevailed until the mid/late 19th Century.

In the 15th Century each tenant of the manor was allowed to keep 2 pigs on the Common but if he failed to "ring and yoke" them by the feast of St Martin (11 November) he could be fined 12 pence (5p or 9 cents) per pig. At the SE corner of the Common, near to the war memorial and the bus-stop on Parkside, there still stands a wooden pound in which stray animals were impounded until their owner paid a fine to release them. The first records of such a pound date from 1617 but its location has moved 2 or 3 times since then.

Tenants also had the right to collect firewood but not to fell trees, except to repair ploughs and carts and to excavate gravel and sand for their own use.

In the middle-ages the "rights of commons" were administered by a special local court meeting 3 or 4 times a year.

In the early 1800's a number of concerned local residents, angered by Earl Spencer's proposal to "enclose" part of the Common and build his new family mansion upon it managed (just) to get his bill thrown out by Parliament. A descendant of his tried again in 1864, and lost again. An Act of Parliament was passed in 1871 "for the preservation of the whole of

Wimbledon Common and Putney Heath, unenclosed, for the benefit of the neighbourhood and public".

The present structure of administration with Commons Conservators was established in 1871 when the Act of Parliament mentioned above required the Spencer family to sell their interest effectively to the nation for a price of £1,200 (US$ 2,150) per annum, payments which finally ended in 1958.

In 1860 the 5th Earl Spencer encouraged the formation of The National Rifle Association to promote marksmanship among soldiers, the better to protect Britain against the threat of invasion by France. He made parts of the Common available as a training area. Queen Victoria attended the inaugural NRA meeting in 1860 and annual meetings on the Common continued for 30 years attracting huge numbers of spectators. In 1889 a local gravedigger was killed by a stray NRA bullet and the ranges were transferred to Bisley. The last annual review was held in 1891 with Kaiser Wilhelm II taking the salute.

The Common has 17 miles (28 km) of bridle paths for horse riders. There are 2 riding schools / livery stables in the Village, one behind the Dog & Fox pub and one on the corner of Ridgway and Hillside, on the West side of the village.

Golf was first played on the Common in 1865. When the Conservators took over the administration of the Common in 1871 they required "every person playing golf to wear a red coat or other red outer garment". To this day the same rule applies to all golfers on the Common.

THE WINDMILL

The best–known "symbol" of rural Wimbledon is the wind-mill on the Common.

The windmill was apparently first thought of by the brewer John Watney, who applied for consent to build it in 1799. It seems he failed to provide any detailed plans so the application was never considered.

The present windmill was built in 1816-17 by one Charles March, a carpenter from nearby Roehampton. It was built as "a public cornmill for the advantage and convenience of the neighbourhood".

From 1838 the miller was also sworn in as a special constable to arrest robbers and was given responsibility for preventing duels from taking place on the Common. The reason for this latter duty seems to have been that the area now occupied by Queensmere Pond was in the early 19th Century a newly-fashionable place to hold duels, taking on this accolade from Putney Heath to the North. Most duels seem to have ended harmlessly but in 1838 there was a death, hence the decision to police the area more vigorously.

In 1840 the miller arrested Lord Cardigan, who subsequently led the charge of the light brigade, for duelling. Cardigan got off "on a technicality" but the case caused so much public uproar that duelling rapidly became unfashionable and there is no record of subsequent duels by pistol in the vicinity of the windmill.

In 1864 the mill was sold to Lord Spencer who removed the millstones and converted the building into cottages to rent. The first tenants of the converted windmill were officials of the National Rifle Association. Baden Powell was a later tenant and during his stay completed his book "*Scouting for Boys*", the "bible" of the Boy Scout movement.

In 1976 after substantial renovation and rebuilding the windmill opened as a museum and is still open to the public today (in the summer only). If you have any time spare before a hard day's tennis-watching you should take a look at it!

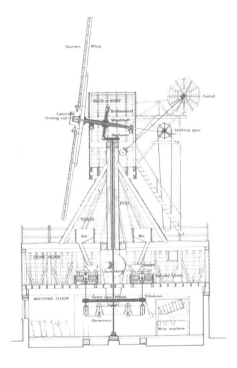

ACKNOWLEDGEMENTS

As you may imagine, there are facts, figures and opinions about Wimbledon, tennis, and its players, in many places. I used all kinds of sources and where opinions differed had to make a choice. I am quite happy to be corrected by my readers and can be contacted at info@ffnf.co.uk

The following sources were particularly helpful:

http://www.wimbledon.org
http://www.tradgames.org.uk
http://www.real-tennis.com
http://www.lta.org.uk/
http://www.itftennis.com/
http://homepage.ntlworld.com/andrew.lemay/bwta.htm
http://www.bbc.co.uk/pressoffice
http://www.espn.go.com/tennis/wimbledon
http://ourworld.cs.com/atomalt/index.htm
http://www.nationmaster.com/encyclopedia/
Wimbledon-championships
http://www.wimbledonmuseum.org.uk
The Book of Tennis by Chris Bowers
http://www.thebookoftennis.com
Many books by Richard Milward
(available from the The Wimbledon Society Museum,
http://www.wimbledonmuseum.org.uk
wimbledonmuseum@yahoo.co.uk)

All author royalties from this book will be donated to The Wimbledon Society Museum (not the tennis museum but the local history one at the corner of Lingfield Rd., SW19).